THE GAP YEAR GUIDE

FAITH BASED PROGRAMS THAT
CHANGE LIVES

LEANN GREGORY

TABLE OF CONTENTS

WHY?

Why Take a Gap Year?

The Dreaded Question

So, what are you doing next year? It's the question asked to most every high school senior at holiday gatherings, in the grocery aisle, and by every well-meaning adult in their lives. And, it's a terrifying question for many of them. Why? Because often they don't *know* their next step, so they must come up with an "acceptable" answer in hopes of avoiding more questions. Usually the answer involves college and a vague reference to a college major they have heard of from a tv show. After all, that is what people expect. But maybe it is time to stop assuming that the next step should always be the most obvious one.

A Different World

It used to be easy to figure out your next step in life. The typical path to adulthood followed a predictable sequence in our society: graduate from high school, finish four years of college, get a job after graduation, get married, start a family.

Whether we consider this sequence right or wrong, it ceases to be the "norm" in the 21st century. Today, online learning, flexible work options, and rapidly changing technological advances open new paths toward the future.

This is both good and bad. The freedom to chart your own course can seem liberating, but following a prescribed path can help teens make decisions and move toward adult responsibility. Choosing a path from limitless options might seem positive - until you actually need to make decisions. I experienced this after living oversesa for 12 years in a country with limited options. Returning to the United States, even a trip to the grocery store to buy cereal was overwhelming. How was I to choose from the hundreds of colorful boxes on the shelf? Each touted benefits: great taste, healthy grains, GMO free. What benefits did I value the most? Taste? Price? Health? Which one was the best for ME?

The same is true for many teens today. When faced with a myriad of options, deciding their next steps can be paralyzing. Most teens opt for the traditional path of applying to college right out of high school in hopes of finding their way there, yet with many colleges offering over 200 majors, this alone doesn't provide a clear path to the future.

Evidence shows that this plethora of choices confuses our students. According to the National Center for Education Statistics, almost 80 percent of students in the United States change their major at least once during their college careers, and many change their major up to three times during that period. To add to the confusion, in 2010 only 62 percent of U.S. college graduates had a job that even required a college degree and only 27 percent had a job closely related to their major. The result? When an 18-year-old looks at all the options and tries to decide where each will lead, they are understandably stressed and confused.

In addition, the path to a college degree has become a very expensive journey. When I attended college in 1986, tuition and fees for one year were $1,323; my complete college education, minus room and board, cost around $5,500. It was possible to work during the semester and throughout the summer to cover my expenses. Today, the same university costs $13,006 a year — much more than a summer job and a few hours of part-time work can cover. Based on current prices, graduation rates today, and adding room and board, books, and other expenses, the full cost is closer to $180,000!

"Average" graduation rates have risen as well. Instead of the traditional four-year standard, the federal government now requires schools to report their "on time" graduation rates based on a six year time frame. Adding two years to an already expensive college degree raises the cost of "finding yourself" in college by more than 150%.

Consumer Reports' August 2016 cover story, "I Kind of Ruined My Life by Going to College," reveals a sad reality for many young adults in America. The accompanying article, "Lives on Hold," shares the story of Jackie Krowen whose $152,000 in student debt has had life-altering effects on her decisions, relationships, and plans for the future. She is not alone. Seventy percent of students now graduate with college debt and enormous loan payments that can prevent them from moving into independent adulthood.

The bottom line - college is a very expensive and confusing place to gain life experience and direction for the future. Before assuming that college is the best next step for students, it is wise to consider other ways to prepare them for what lies ahead in their lives. Perhaps students need a break from the classroom before making decisions about how they will invest the tens of thousands of dollars a college education will cost.

The Status Quo

The world today is far different from the one in which we, the parents, grew up. While we bought textbooks and attended college classes to gain information from knowledgeable professors, students now log on to their computers and search for anything they need to know. If they don't feel like reading, they can watch a YouTube video. If they don't like the perspective they find, they can simply find another "expert" online. If they need bolstering that their idea is the best, it isn't difficult to find a Facebook group of people who agree. The reality is this: students are not short on information, but they lack wisdom for applying this information to real life situations.

Few have studied Generation Y more than Tim Elmore of Growing Leaders, a character and leadership development company. In his book *Artificial Maturity*, Elmore explains how teens have overexposure to information yet underexposure to genuine life experience. The application of "head" knowledge has been lost, thus creating false confidence in our teens. This same condition can be found in the church as well. While teens may have heard great sermons or listened to inspiring podcasts, many haven't experienced a testing of their faith. True confidence comes from knowing they can solve the problems they encounter via life experience.

The Downside of Convenience

Certainly, technology makes our lives more convenient, but is that always good?

Elmore notes, "Our world has become so convenient, instant, simple and virtual that certain intellectual, emotional, relational and spiritual muscles atrophy because they don't get exercised."

Students often lack virtues that are crucial to healthy adulthood like:

- **Patience/delayed gratification** - the ability to wait on a reward that comes slowly
- **Connection/people skills** - the ability to build common ground with those unlike you
- **Responsibility/morals and ethics** - the ability to do what's right even when acting alone
- **Endurance/tenacity** - the ability to stay committed and complete work toward a goal
- **Empathy** - the ability to understand and share the feelings of another

Many of these virtues are not reflected in a student's book knowledge or IQ but by their Emotional Intelligence Quotient, or EQ.

The Need for Emotional Intelligence

The concept of Emotional Intelligence was first proposed in the early 1990's by John Mayer of the University of New Hampshire and Yale professor Peter Salovey and later popularized by *New York Times* bestselling author Daniel Goleman in *Emotional Intelligence*.

The Institute for Health and Human Potential defines emotional intelligence as "awareness that emotions can drive behavior and impact people both positively or negatively and that learning to manage emotions is vital." According to Goleman, there are five key elements to emotional intelligence: self-awareness, self-regulation, motivation, empathy, and social skills.

A good gap year program focuses on developing these areas and building the virtues of patience, responsibility, and tenacity which, in turn, develops a student's EQ. This, in turn, leads them towards success in college, their personal lives, and their future careers. Additionally, a strong EQ helps students acquire the skills and attributes that colleges and employers look for: maturity, confidence, problem-solving, communications skills, and independence.

The Importance of Self-Awareness

In addition to developing emotional intelligence, teens need time to develop a clear sense of their strengths, natural gifts, and passions. Many kids are told from a young age that they are good at everything. In an effort to build self esteem, parents, teachers, and coaches often applaud every effort and honor every student. Everyone gets a trophy! While the heart behind this is admirable, the results can be damaging. When students believe they can be anything they want to be, they are set up for real disappointment when, as young adults, others surpass them in skill and ability.

Having a realistic view of their strengths and weaknesses will help students find direction for their lives and focus their efforts in areas in which they will excel. Let's face it, most high school students are unable to articulate their true strengths and weaknesses. If you have a teen who has tried to fill out an application of any kind they have probably asked you, "Mom, what should I put for my strengths and weaknesses?" Students need time, life experiences, and honest mentors to help them become more self-aware. A well-planned gap year can provide these things.

If you are raising teenagers, you know how hard it can be for them to look beyond the task at hand (pass the test, make the team, get the date). Yet, as adults, we know that stepping outside of our own needs and becoming more aware of the "bigger picture" is crucial to maturity. In a world where living for yourself is encouraged, gaining a perspective of living beyond yourself can be hard for students. Placing them in environments where they are not the center of their own world helps them see a bigger picture and find their place in it.

The Need for Spiritual Development

A 2018 report from Barna Group, a faith-based research organization, reveals a trend in Generation Z (students born between 1994 and 2012) toward relative truth and away from church involvement with more than half of respondents saying that church involvement is "not too" or "not at all" important to them. According to the study, 34 percent of Gen Z's religious affiliation is either atheist, agnostic, or none; teens 13 to 18 years old are twice as likely as adults to say they are atheists; and 59 percent of 13 to 18 year olds say they are some kind of Christian.

When it comes to morality, a mere 34 percent of Gen Z agrees that lying is morally wrong while 24 percent say what is morally right and wrong changes over time based on society. Pluralism has influenced this generation vastly, and 58 percent of those polled agree with the statement, "Many religions can lead to eternal life; there is no 'one true religion'."

In light of this research, I believe there are two elements that are vital when preparing Gen Z for the future. First, they need time as young adults to study, contemplate, discuss, and even challenge the beliefs they were taught at home and in church. This is of critical importance if they plan to go to a secular college where their faith will be challenged daily, but I believe that it is just as important if they are headed into the job market, ministry, or parenting. Teens need to *own* their faith, not just subscribe to it because mom and dad, " said so." Exposing them to engaging, inspiring teaching and study of the Bible in a focussed environment can help prepare them for the barrage of perspectives they will be exposed to in our increasingly pluralistic culture. Doing this with peers can make it even more powerful. I often remind my kids that "we match the strides of those we walk with." Being surrounded by other motivated teens can propel our kids forward by leaps and bounds. While living in a "holy huddle" (as we used to call it in campus ministry) is not the real Christian life, taking time away to focus on spiritual growth *is* a wise choice. All of the gap year programs featured in this guide place a priority on solid Biblical teaching and the development of a Christian worldview. You will not find this focus in secular gap year programs.

The second element that is vital in preparing Gen Z for the future is exposing them to new environments and people that will challenge their perceptions of the world around them. Let's face it, many Christian teens are unprepared for the world that awaits them. Jonathan Morrow, Director of Cultural Engagement at Impact 360 Institute, points out, "With the best of intentions, we bubble wrap our kids and create Disney World–like environments for them in our churches, and then wonder why they have no resilience in faith or life. Students are entertained but not prepared. They've had a lot of fun but are not ready to lead."

Placing teens in a new and different environment, one that stretches both their faith and practice, builds a resilience that will help them succeed as adults. While teens' natural instincts are to rely on their own skills and talents, being in unfamiliar places where they are not in control forces them to depend on God. They will likely realize that the coping mechanisms gained in an American Sunday school class will not work in a village in Africa or a homeless shelter in Chicago. Being exposed to the downtrodden and shifting their attention to those in need can teach them that, in the end, the poor give to us and not the other way around. These experiences can bring a completely new perspective to students who have only practiced their faith in "safe" environments.

Is college the best "next step" for everyone?

When we consider ways life is different today from 25 years ago, we need to be open to new avenues that help our kids successfully transition into independent adulthood. (This means moving out of the basement, getting their own insurance and cell phone plan and supporting themselves with a job - among other things!) As we've seen, however, life after high school is far more complex now than it was in the late 80's and early 90's. The path isn't as clear and the options are almost limitless, and many kids are getting stuck. While many parents have assumed that college is the obligatory next step, this may not be the case anymore.

In an interview for the journal of the American Family Association, gap year expert Derek Melleby suggests, "College isn't for everyone. My hunch is that when all of the current research being done on college transition is finished, the solution to the problem of students transitioning poorly will be simple, but most people won't do it. If you want students to transition well and make the most of their college experience, students should strongly consider not going to college immediately after high school. More and more 18-year-

13

olds are not developmentally ready — emotionally, intellectually, and spiritually — for college. Not to mention the financial burden that college brings. Not going to college or taking some time off before going to college should seriously be considered."

Perhaps we need to reevaluate the assumed path and find the one that is right for each individual child. An honest assessment may lead to options including a four-year college, a technical degree, or entrepreneurship, but an assessment isn't *complete* unless the gap year is considered as a way to determine a fitting future path. A well planned gap year can make a life changing impact on our teen's future and give them priceless insight into God's plans for their life. However, it will be effective only if it is done well and with thought and foresight. For this, we need a clear understanding of what a gap year *is* and what it is *not*.

WHAT?

What a Gap Year is and What a Gap Year is Not

A gap year is *not* a year off. According to the Gap Year Association, "A gap year is an experiential semester or year "on", typically taken between high school and college in order to deepen practical, professional, and personal awareness."

To be meaningful, a gap year must be more than a nine-month vacation from school while living off of mom and dad, and it must be intentional - with students learning, working, teaching, traveling, volunteering, exploring professional interests, developing a robust worldview, or any other educational experience. Each of these endeavors offers educational opportunities outside of a traditional classroom while allowing — even demanding — personal development.

A Short History of Gap Years

A gap year is not a new concept. The idea of complementing classroom study with real-world experience dates back to the

17th century when students from elite British families would complete their education by taking a "grand tour" to see firsthand the museums, architecture, and fashion they'd learned about in the classroom. Gap years continued in the U.K. in the 1970's as a way for students to fill the "gap" between final exams and the start of their higher educations.

Students in Great Britain and other countries commonly take a year to gain real-life awareness before attending university. The idea is not as common in the United States but garnered attention in 2016 when Malia Obama took a gap year before entering Harvard, placing her among the estimated 30,000 to 40,000 US students annually who take a planned gap year. This is a number that has increased up to 30% since 2006.

The Gap Year Association promotes dozens of organized gap year programs and states on its website their aim to "advance the field of gap years because we have seen their profound benefits on students from all backgrounds, and believe an intentional gap year can be part of the welfare for us, our nation, our neighbors, and our fellow global citizens."

The Impact of a Gap Year

In 2015, the Gap Year Association published their National Alumni Survey which looks at both demographics and results of gap year programs and participants. Their findings were encouraging:

- 90% of students surveyed enrolled in a four-year institution within one-year of completing their gap year
- Compared to national averages, "Gappers" had lower average time-to-graduation rates (four years or less compared nationally to 59% graduating within six years)
- 86% of the respondents were satisfied or very satisfied with their jobs compared to less than half of US workers who say they are satisfied with their jobs
- 89% participated in community service in the past month while the average US volunteer rate was 25.3 percent for the year ending in September 2014
- Gapper grades in college skew higher

The study concluded that gap years taken before college may help students focus and better select college study plans, reducing the likelihood of transferring schools or changing majors while in college, and as a result, save thousands of dollars.

Most parents are pleasantly surprised to know that schools like Harvard, Princeton, and UNC actually *encourage* students to take time off. In 2009, a near-record 107 of the 1,665 Harvard freshmen had taken a gap year.

> "Harvard College encourages admitted students to defer enrollment for one year to travel, pursue a special project or activity, work, or spend time in another meaningful way — provided they do not enroll in a degree-granting program at another college. Deferrals for two-year obligatory military service are also granted. Each year, between 80 and 110 students defer their matriculation to the College."

The University of North Carolina at Chapel Hill will begin offering 21 Global Gap Year Fellowships in 2020. Students selected for the program will receive an $8,000-$16,000 scholarship towards their gap year.

> "The Global Gap Year Fellowship at UNC-Chapel Hill is the first college-sponsored gap year program that allows students to design their own experience or join Global Citizen Year for a year abroad. The Fellowship partners with UNC-CH Office of Undergraduate Admissions, which helps promote the program and select the recipients, and works with students as they follow their passions working with an international community."

Former Middlebury College Dean of Admissions Bob Clagett say this, "Stepping off the educational treadmill for six months or a year between high school and college can be an important way to remind themselves of what their education should really be about. It can also lead to a much more productive experience once they are enrolled in college, since those students will frequently be more mature, more focused, and more aware of what they want to do with their college education."

An Indulgence of the Elite?

When you read the research, it undeniably points to the benefits of gap year programs, yet many families remain unfamiliar with the idea. Those that are more familiar with gap years often see the programs as an indulgence of the elite, and for good reason. Gap year programs traditionally have been marketed to an elite audience, and many programs look more like expensive vacations around the world rather than educational or volunteer-minded experiences.

While the benefits of world travel are undeniable, we must keep in mind that travel alone will not transform students in ways that matter. Without intentionality and excellent mentorship, a gap year can simply increase a student's sense of entitlement and privilege instead of transforming their perspective and encouraging greater responsibility and maturity.

When our family researched gap year programs several years ago, we looked for something that would impact our children in areas that we felt were crucial to their development into healthy adults: self-awareness, confidence, problem solving, communications skills, independence, and a well-defined world view. We sought environments that would promote spiritual and emotional development as well as opportunities to help them identify their unique gifts and interests. To our surprise, we found a number of excellent Christian gap year programs dedicated to helping students mature in these ways. This newer breed of gap year programs is accessible to a broader audience as many allow (and even encourage) fundraising, accept financial aid, or offer scholarships.

How Christian gap year programs are different

Christian gap year programs in the United States are rather new. While programs like YWAM and Torchbearers International had year-long Bible and ministry schools around the world in the 50's and 60's that students used as gap years, there are a growing number of new programs springing up around the United States. These programs hold some things in common with their secular counterparts; many include travel and volunteer work, but they also have additional goals.

Impact 360 states their goals this way, "Because all truth is God's truth, we reject the idea that reality is to be carved up into the artificial categories of sacred and secular. As Christ-followers, we are called to live every aspect of our lives under God's authority and for God's glory. There should not be a disconnect between how we think and how we live. This educational philosophy is bolstered by the three pillars of our program: Know. Be. Live."

Vox Bivium (whose name means "the voice at the crossroads") looks for high school graduates who accept the quest to gain better clarity and understanding for who they truly are and what God has called them to do. Their program provides guidance for those who seek the junction where their "deep gladness and the world's deep hunger meet," where they learn what they most need to do and what the world needs most to have done.

The mission of One Life gap year is to launch and develop servant leaders who live out their faith in every area of life. They believe that in order to grow in character you must first truly examine who you are becoming. As a result there is a strong focus on studying God's word, while living in deep

Christian community, so that you can discern your place in the will of God.

It is clear that programs like these have very distinct goals related to the development of Christian character while still including some of the effective elements of secular programs like travel and volunteer work. In my opinion this makes Christian gap year programs stand out among all others and be a priceless investment in our student's lives. Yet, I know that there are many questions that arise when parents first consider a gap year for their child. I will seek to answer the most frequent ones here.

Parents' Most Frequent Questions Answered

Veering from a traditional path can be scary both for students and parents. In my experience, however, it's the parents who have the most questions. Will their student come back from a gap year and start college? Will the delay prevent them from doing well in school? Will they lose scholarship money? Is it dangerous for students this age to travel? These are all legitimate concerns I have heard from parents in recent years. Here are answers to some of the most common questions I am asked:

Does taking a gap year make it harder for students to go back to school and study again?

In *Gap Year: How Delaying College Changes People in Ways the World Needs*, Joe O'Shea cites the following studies:

> "In Australia and the United Kingdom, economic researchers found that high school students who deferred their admission to college to take a Gap Year went to college (after their gap year) at the same rate as those who

accepted an offer and intended to go straight there (Birch and Miller 2007; Crawford and Cribb 2012). In fact, in the United Kingdom and in the United States, students who had taken a Gap Year were more likely to graduate with higher grade point averages than observationally identical individuals who went straight to college, and this effect was seen even for gap year students with lower academic achievement in high school."

A gap year can actually motivate a student to work harder in college and finish at a quicker rate than their peers. Why? When a student spends time working during their gap year and/or paying their own expenses, they will likely gain motivation to pursue a career that will help them meet their real-life expenses in a more efficient manner. Further, they will discover things they *do* and *don't* like about a job or internship, which will assist them in choosing a path they really care about. They also will be exposed to people who are farther down the path of life (other than mom and dad) who can speak wisdom into their lives and point out their strengths and weaknesses. And yes, some students finish a gap year and decide not to pursue a college degree. But, in this case we must question if they had the motivation to begin with. Maybe they should seek a different path altogether.

What about applying to college?

Parents and their students often wonder if they should apply for college with their peers or wait until after their gap year. For the majority of students, it is best to apply while they are still in high school. Because of the momentum created by senior year, it can be easier to focus and evaluate next steps than when you are immersed in a gap year and potentially in a place without internet! Additionally, students have ready access to school counselors and resources during their junior and senior years that can help in their college searches and to teachers who can write the needed recommendations. Sometimes students are not ready to apply to college immediately and need more time to process the decision. If the gap year takes place primarily in the US, it may be possible to complete the college application process while enrolled in the program. Just make sure your student is aware of deadlines and admission requirements for the schools they decide to pursue.

What is deferred enrollment?

After acceptance into a university, students can speak with the admissions office about deferring enrollment. Most admissions offices grant deferrals to students pursuing a gap year, however it's advisable to discuss this with the school sooner rather than later, preferably between April and June. The Gap Year Association website provides informal information on the specific deferral processes of hundreds of American colleges and universities but always contact your specific college or university for their most updated policies and procedures.

Can a student earn college credit during a gap year?

Many gap year programs now include college credit through partner universities. Students enroll with the partner school's online program and earn credits that later can be transferred to the college they plan to attend after their gap year. There are two sides to this coin. Earning college credits is great and helps a student get ahead, however this route can impact enrollment status and affect financial aid and scholarships. Because the student is "enrolled" in the college associated with the gap program, the university they apply to enter following their gap year may consider them a transfer student. Be sure to check with the school to see if earning college credit during a gap year is allowed.

There is a clearer answer for students who have already been accepted into a particular college and deferred enrollment, they often are not allowed to earn credit during the gap year.

The reason for this is that when students accept admission and then defer enrollment, they are making an agreement with their college. The school agrees to hold a spot on campus and not offer it to someone else and the student agrees to come back and be a full member of the student body following their gap year.

What do college admissions offices think of gap years?

While many colleges and universities actually recommend gap years, the still-low percentage of American high school seniors taking them means plenty of schools are unfamiliar with the concept. Once your student decides to take a gap year and defer from a specific school, it's advisable to call the admissions and financial aid offices to discuss how this decision will affect enrollment. Helping people understand the gap year often leads them to let go of their biggest concerns.

Will my student get "behind" by taking a gap year?

If sticking with high school friends is important to a student, a gap year will put them "behind" in a sense. However, it also puts them ahead. How? Students may end up with less college credit after a gap year, but they will gain life experience that can help them make more informed decisions about their future and achieve their goals in a more efficient manner.

Most parents don't realize that "average" graduation rates are now calculated at six years rather than four. On average, students are taking longer to graduate. This is often due to the lack of clear goals. According to a report from the Education Department's National Center for Education Statistics, almost a third of first-time college students change their majors at least once in the first three years of college. In addition, a 2015 report by the National Student Clearinghouse Research Center found that 37.2 percent of college students change schools at least once within six years and, of these, 45 percent changed their institution more than once. These factors obviously increase the length of time it takes to finish a degree since credit hours are lost and new classes are needed. This also increases the already high cost of college by up to 150 percent.

Therefore, it is unlikely that a gap year will put your student "behind." It is more likely to provide direction that will help them earn their degree in a more efficient and timely manner. And, if a student returns from a gap year without clear direction, it may not be the right time to invest in an expensive education anyway.

Did you know?

One way to "get ahead" so that your gap year won't put you behind your peers in college is to earn college credit while still in high school. Whether you do this through dual enrollment, CLEP testing, AP exams or other options, you can earn up to 60 hours of credit, which equals two years of school. To learn more about this option, I highly recommend Jennifer Cook-DeRosa's book *Homeschooling for College Credit*. Even if you aren't homeschooling throughout high school, the book illustrates the ways you can maximize high school years to earn college credit before high school graduation.

Will my student lose financial aid?

Every school differs in the ways they handle gap years. While almost all colleges in the U.S. allow students to defer for a gap year, financial aid and scholarship policies vary.

Because federal financial aid must be re-applied for each year, a gap year likely will not affect financial aid awards unless your family has a major shift in financial status. Some gap year programs (ones that offer 24+ hours of college credit) accept federal financial aid. The Free Application for Student Aid (FAFSA) is available on October 1st each year and I recommend that parents fill out the FAFSA as soon as it is available. The information comes from the parents' previous year's taxes. If a student is not earning college credit during their gap year they should wait to fill out the FAFSA forms until they apply to college.

Will a gap year cause a student to lose scholarship opportunities?

Eight states have lottery scholarship programs that provide tuition scholarships to qualifying students and all but three allow students to defer their enrollment by at least 16 months.

State	Name of program	Enrollment window
TN	Tennessee HOPE	16 months
TN	Tennessee Promise	Immediate
AR	Academic Challenge	Immediate
FL	Bright Futures/FMS	3 years
GA	HOPE, Zell Miller	No limit
KY	KEES	5 years
NM	Legislative lottery	Immediate
SC	HOPE, LIFE, Palmetto	No limit
WV	PROMISE	2 years

Several states and cities offer free tuition for community college classes. Each program is different, but some require immediate enrollment. For example, the Tennessee Promise program requires that students "attend full-time and continuously at an eligible postsecondary institution in the fall term immediately following graduation." As a result, participating in a gap year program disqualifies you from the Tennessee Promise Scholarship. Policies change frequently, so it is necessary to check with the program your student is interested in before applying to a gap year.

Merit-based scholarships

Merit-based scholarships often can be deferred, but be sure to confirm guidelines with the scholarship administrators. A well-explained gap year can actually help students receive merit scholarships. If a student articulates the ways in which a gap year will help them learn and grow as a person and how it will make them a better student, they can set themselves apart from applicants who plan to attend college directly after high school. Since only two to five percent of students currently take a gap year in the U.S., this can be a compelling factor in winning scholarships.

Is it dangerous?

As parents, the transition of students from childhood to adulthood is difficult. Our tendency to avoid risk and quickly come to the rescue of our students when they face difficulties is strong. Keeping them on the prescribed path or bailing them out financially when they make a bad decision may alleviate our anxiety, but these things do not encourage their growth. Students need to own their problems and experience challenges that cause them to mature. When calling mom is not an option, it is amazing the problems our kids can solve.

The world can be a dangerous place whether at a concert in the U.S. or on a train in Paris. Let's be honest, no one can guarantee the complete safety of anyone anywhere, so students need to take common sense precautions. Most organized gap year programs have team leaders trained in basic areas of crisis management with contingency plans developed for each location. This is an important thing to ask as you are considering various programs and opportunities.

We need to be sure, however, that we are not being overprotective of our student because of our own fears. We didn't keep them in diapers until high school and we don't want to treat them like adolescents when they are moving toward independent adulthood.

How will we pay for a gap year?

If you choose to participate in an organized program, you can expect to pay $10,000 to $20,000 over the course of nine months. Some programs only last one semester, allowing the student to work the other semester to help finance the program. Other programs encourage fundraising and train students to effectively raise funding for their gap year. For example, Adventures in Missions helps students raise all of the money they need to cover their nine months of travel and ministry. Cru (formerly Campus Crusade for Christ) coaches students in support-raising as well.

Additionally, there are programs that offer financial assistance to students. My son received a very generous financial aid package from Impact 360 bringing the cost of his gap year down significantly. Because the Impact 360 program offers college credit through Union University, he also was able to apply a $2,500 Remarkable Futures scholarship that he won from Chick-fil-A toward that portion of his gap year expenses.

If a gap year offers 24 hours of college credit or more, students qualify for federal student aid and can apply with FAFSA (The Free Application for Federal Student Aid). Several programs in this guide offer this option. In addition, when credit if offered through a qualified institution, students may be able to use money saved in a 529 savings plan.

Keep in mind, a well-planned gap year is an investment in your child's future. The money that is spent for a quality program will likely yield a dividend that far surpasses the cost.

Additionally, if your student enters college with greater focus and direction, you will likely pay less for their education.

Can you take a gap year if you already completed a year of college?

Absolutely! Almost every program mentioned in this guide allows students to participate even if they have already completed a year (or more) of college. If your student is struggling with motivation in college, or unsure of the direction they want to take afterwards, then a gap year could be a great opportunity to take a break and re-evaluate.

Is it wrong to push my child to do a gap year?

What if you think a gap year would be a great idea but your child isn't sold on it? This is a tricky question. There are many things we push our child to do because we know it is in their best interest; exercise, study, brush their teeth....the list goes on. The reality is that many 17 year olds do not have the foresight to make wise decisions for the future. Perhaps this is why we see so many of them amassing paralyzing debt, changing their major multiple times, and seeing college as more of a 4 year party than preparation for the future.

Teens rarely react well to having something pushed on them, but using discretion and wisdom on your part can often influence their decision. Focus on the things they will experience in a gap year. Teens generally like to do things that are "outside the box" - so capitalize on that. Take them to visit the program and meet some of the students. Our overnight visit to Impact 360 sealed the deal with our son. When he had a chance to spend time with current students, see the amazing facility, and hear other guys say, "My mom wanted me to do this, but it has already been the best 3 months of my life" he began to get excited about the possibility. In addition, most of the programs mentioned in this guide have excellent websites aimed at teens and active social media accounts that share their adventures. AIM's World Race gap year does an amazing job at recruitment through social media. After all, who doesn't want their picture made with an elephant in India, or a selfie at the Taj Mahal? Encourage your teens to read the blogs of current and former participants and follow their Instagram accounts to get a better idea of what a gap year can look like. You can find the links to these accounts in the program profile section of this guide.

How do I choose a program?

Students first need to determine their purpose in taking a gap year. Do they need a break from formal academics? Is there a specific skill they hope to develop? Do they need more time to mature emotionally or socially before college? Are they itching to see the world? Different programs will appeal to different interests. All the programs in this guide have a goal of developing students spiritually in one way or another. However, some do this by immersing them in new environments that are completely unfamiliar while others take place in a more academic classroom setting. Some programs are very small, with only 10-20 students each year, while others are large, sending 250 teens around the world. Sit down with your teen and consider what type of environment they would thrive in and what type of learning excites them. Of course, you will want to be sure you agree with the program's philosophy and theological viewpoint before you commit. All of the programs listed in this guide provide excellent information on their websites to help answer these questions.

Are there good reasons NOT to take a gap year?

Yes. If a student is struggling emotionally a gap year is not a good place to try to work through these issues. These opportunities are not designed as counseling programs and a student who is struggling would be better off spending time in professional counseling at home under the supervision of parents or loved ones.

In addition, some students need the momentum to continue their education that is found in a direct entrance into college. Delaying their entrance could potentially leave them unmotivated to continue their education. If it is important to you that they complete a degree, you may want to keep them on the path with their peers. If you are open to them finding an alternate path, should they so choose, then go ahead with the gap year. It is difficult to know exactly how the year will impact their decisions about the future, but most come out with a clearer understanding of themselves as well as more clarity and direction for the lives.

Components of an Effective Gap Year

When considering the idea of a gap year, it is important to know what to look for in an effective program. If you choose to design your own gap year, it needs to be designed with the same level of intentionality found in the structured programs featured in this guide. In light of the needs of this generation of students, I believe that an effective gap year of *any* type needs to include some or all of the following: structure, focused learning, appropriate risk, a feedback-rich environment, an unfamiliar setting, and a diverse audience. A Christian gap year should also include: solid Biblical teaching and mentorship, like minded peers, and ministry opportunities.

Structure

The biggest mistake families make when planning a gap year is lack of structure. "Figuring it out as you go" is not a good plan. When August rolls around and friends head to college and begin posting pictures of their cute dorm room and freshman welcome parties, students who are still home "figuring out" their gap year can feel like they are missing out and begin doubting their decision.

You can avoid this problem by creating a clear plan during a student's senior year that begins at the same time as their peers leave for college. If the gap year includes travel, which I highly recommend, this is a great time for their travel to begin. Even if a student plans to work part of the gap year, perhaps travelling first is still a good idea. While friends are sharing their new and exciting experiences on social media, gap year students will have their own unique experiences to share as well. Whether designing your own gap year or participating in a program, having a structure in place sets students up for the best experience.

Focused Learning

A gap year is not the time to stop learning! In fact, it's the perfect opportunity to learn in ways that a busy high school schedule probably didn't allow. Whether it be acquiring a new skill, reading more from a favorite author, taking a painting class, learning to cook, completing a financial literacy course, or studying scripture, a gap year provides the margin students need to focus on something other than strictly academic pursuits.

For families and students interested in spiritual development as we were, the opportunity to develop a Christian worldview before heading off to a secular university is compelling. Possessing a Christian worldview will help students base their future decisions on a solid foundation rather than the shifting sands of our culture. What is a worldview? Jonathan Morrow, author and Christian worldview coach, explains, "A worldview is a web of habit-forming beliefs about the biggest questions of life that helps you make sense of all your experiences." Everyone has a worldview whether they can articulate it or not. Having a worldview that is consistent with your faith and based on truth provides the ultimate road map to the future. If a student can answer the questions of "Who am I?" and "Why am I here?" they are more likely to have clarity as they step into the future.

Appropriate Risk Coupled with Appropriate Responsibility

We live in a risk-averse age where we, as parents, often swoop in to "save the day" when something goes wrong for our child. We call a teacher about a student's bad grade or fill out college application papers for our high schooler. I know, because I have done my share of "saving the day." We love our kids and we want them to succeed, but protecting our kids from negative or difficult experiences handicaps them from assuming adult responsibilities. We end up protecting them from the consequences of bad choices that prevent them from making better ones in the future. They need to learn, via experience, the consequences of certain behaviors. They need to take ownership of their lives.

Author Tim Elmore says it well, "Taking calculated risks is all a part of growing up. In fact, it plays a huge role. Childhood may be about safety and self-esteem, but as a student matures, risk and achievement are necessities in forming their identity and confidence. Because parents have removed 'risk' from children's lives, psychologists are using a term as they counsel teens: High Arrogance, Low Self-Esteem. They are cocky, but deep down their confidence is hollow, it's built off of watching YouTube videos, and perhaps not really achieving something meaningful."

A gap year presents students with age appropriate risks. In preparation for her gap year, my daughter needed to raise $16,000, no small feat. It was a scary prospect for my husband and I as parents and for her as an 18-year-old. We could have called grandparents and asked for a loan or taken out a second mortgage on our house to pay for the program, but we didn't. Our daughter wrote letters, made phone calls, spoke to groups, and was creative in finding and asking for help in funding her trip. She learned to articulate her needs, to speak with strangers and family friends, and to take initiative towards her goal. It was the first big step of faith in what would turn out to be a year of risks and rewards. The result was a newfound confidence that continues to put other scary tasks she faces into perspective and encourages her to take appropriate risks and responsibility in her life.

Becoming a contributor and not just a consumer is a crucial part of growing up. In my opinion, too many teens are given tremendous privilege with very little responsibility. I only have to drive around the parking lot of the local high school to see dozens of shiny new cars driven by 16-18 year olds. In our family, we insist that our kids pay for half of their first car, and we match their savings up to $2,500. In case you are wondering, our kids *don't* like this plan. They don't understand why other parents buy their kids nice *new* cars while we make them buy their own *used* car? (The nerve!) We also require them to pay for their gas and half of their insurance. As a result they all had to get part time jobs to help contribute to their expenses - that's responsibility. We see it as a vital part of their education.

The reality is that many teens today don't have part-time jobs like most of us did in the 80's, and why should they? When a completely comfy lifestyle is supported by parents with very little contribution from the student it is no wonder that they go to college and waste both time and money on their education. We need to help them see that life in the "real world" costs money, this is crucial in developing their sense of responsibility and removing their sense of entitlement.

A gap year provides many opportunities for both risk and responsibility. Risk can be accomplished through travel to new places, working in new environments, trying new activities, and developing new skills. Responsibility is gained as students live away from home and are in charge of their finances, relationships, and schedules.

A Feedback-Rich Environment

To truly grow, people need feedback. This can be difficult for students who have heard they can "be anything they want to be" or that they are "the best" at everything. Part of growing into adulthood is understanding your unique strengths as well as your limitations and weaknesses. Several tools can help students understand themselves better. When I coach a students, I have them take personality tests like Myers Briggs or the DISC to help them articulate their strengths and weaknesses. The Clifton Strengths assessment — formally StrengthsFinder — or the Enneagram are also helpful tools for self-awareness. Good gap year programs incorporate these tools into their curriculum to help students become more self aware.

While tests and assessments can help identify patterns and tendencies, there is no substitute for friends and mentors willing to give real-time feedback and challenge. One of the hardest parts of my daughter's gap year was the weekly "feedback" time when her team of seven came together to give and receive feedback from the week. Instead of harboring bitterness or practicing conflict avoidance, they were forced to "get it out into the open". I won't lie, she didn't love it, but I have noticed a pronounced difference in her awareness of her emotions and her empathy toward others' struggles since she has returned.

Peers can provide valuable feedback that leads to growth, but I believe students also need someone who can provide both mentoring and accountability. These relationships are generally most effective with someone who is farther down the path of life. A person with life experience and wisdom can provide invaluable guidance to a young person who is willing to learn from someone else's mistakes and victories. While it may be easier to sit in an audience and try to learn, evidence proves that just attending church or a class lecture does not work. Mentoring relationships provide a more effective environment for growth. Author and speaker Gordon

MacDonald says, "Mature Christians don't grow through programs or through the mesmerizing delivery of a talented speaker or worship band. Would-be saints are mentored one-on-one or, better yet, one-on-small group — three to twelve was Jesus' model. Mature Christians are made one-by-one through the influence of other Christians already mature." A gap year that can provide a mature mentor is priceless.

An Unfamiliar Setting

Have you ever noticed that putting yourself in a new environment, culture, or work setting heightens awareness of your assumptions and the habits and customs of others? Experiencing something new awakens our senses and increases our understanding of ourselves. For a gap year to be transformational, it must be distinct from the student's past experiences and require them to face new challenges. Being forced to solve real-world problems is exactly what is needed to increase confidence. Putting ourselves in unfamiliar settings can cause us to grow in ways we don't experience in our day-to-day lives. This is especially true for students, as their limited life experience often does not provide opportunities to immerse themselves in unfamiliar settings.

Travelling and experiencing different cultures is a component in most every great gap year program. Programs featured in this guide take students to Israel, Brazil, Swaziland, Nepal and beyond. This stretches students in ways their typical high school experience did not, even if it was through homeschool. Whether the experience is for a few weeks or for the entire year, students come away changed.

A Diverse Audience

Many high school students spend the majority of their time with their peers. This is especially true for public school students in America who spend approximately 1,000 hours in school per year. Add the time involved in after-school activities or simply hanging out with their friends and the hours multiply. With teens' propensities to gravitate towards those who are most like them, it's easy for them to get stuck in "group think." This is the practice of thinking or making decisions as a group in a manner that discourages creativity or individual responsibility.

Homeschool parents have long recognized that exposure to a variety of age groups and people offers tremendous benefits to their student. For one, students who are exposed to multigenerational environments often have better communication skills. (After all, grandma probably doesn't use SnapChat.) When they are primarily socializing with peers they communicate in the ways that are common to their age group.

I'm still surprised to see teens using their phones to text one another when they are in the same room! They often lack opportunity (and motivation) to make eye contact and talk to others face-to-face. As a result, many of them lack crucial social skills in this area. It is easy to see how this can make job interviews challenging. Choosing a gap year that exposes teens to a variety of people, spanning all ages, helps develop empathy, communication skills, and perspective in ways that traditional schooling cannot.

In addition, many middle-class Americans live in neighborhoods and attend churches that are racially homogeneous and don't afford students the opportunity to work or worship with members of other cultures, countries, or traditions. Most teens have never met people suffering from extreme poverty or living in conditions that most Americans would find deplorable. Yet, it is these very experiences that change students, motivating them to make the world a kinder, better place and possibly even helping them decide to apply their talents towards building communities and initiating change.

Exposing students to diversity, whether it be generational, racial, or economic develops better citizens, better employees, and better people. A gap year is the perfect opportunity to introduce this diversity to students. Seek out opportunities that expose your student to people who are different from those they normally encounter in their lives.

The Context of a
Transformational Gap Year

Structure, learning, risk, feedback, diversity. If these are the components which make a gap year transformational, where should it take place? The good news is that these elements can be gained in a variety of settings and through a wide range of experiences. For many, this involves travel, but it can also be found through meaningful work or a structured gap year program.

Travel

Because travel exposes students to unfamiliar cultures and traditions while involving risk and new experiences, it is a vital part of an effective gap year. When students are exposed to people different from themselves, their beliefs and assumptions about the world are challenged, and they must evaluate their beliefs and why they have them. When done in connection with Godly mentors and a firm foundation in the Bible, students come away strengthened in their faith.

In addition, travel requires students to be more independent because they can't rely on mom and dad to help them catch the next bus or train or to manage their money for them. Yes, they may end up in some sticky situations, but they will develop the skills to navigate the world around them. These skills will be invaluable in developing both confidence and problem solving abilities that will prove useful down the road.

A word of caution

If travel is the primary way a student will spend their gap year, it is important that they have some type of mentor relationship to help them navigate and evaluate their experiences. A program team leader, a believer living in the foreign country, or a church contact will provide a mature adult speaking into students' lives, thus helping them understand themselves better and encouraging them to grow and change in meaningful ways. Simply taking a trip to a foreign country will not result in the life changes that are hoped for otherwise. Vacations do not have the same effect as time spent living with locals, and international experiences can be difficult to interpret and learn from when they are not paired with the wisdom of a mentor.

Work

Many of the components of an effective gap year can also be incorporated through work, whether it be volunteer, paid, or an internship. If work or an internship are part of a student's gap year, it will be most effective if the student finds an experience that is totally unfamiliar, forcing them to navigate uncertain situations and perhaps even fail occasionally. Additionally, working in a multigenerational setting also encourages students' growth. While it may be fun to work in a coffee shop with their peers, working with people who have more life experience can be priceless.

Another benefit of working during a gap year is that students are exposed to new career fields and gain a more realistic picture of what a particular career might involve. Watching *Grey's Anatomy* and deciding to be a nurse is much different than working in a nursing home. These experiences can save thousands of dollars when a student enters college more informed about the major they are pursuing. While most students pursue careers they have only read about or seen on TV, your student will have real-world experience backing up his or her choice.

Structured Programs

Great gap years don't just happen. They are well-planned, strategic investments in a student's growth and development. Selecting or designing a program that fits your desired goals leads to an experience that is much more likely to be transformational. Fortunately, there are a growing number of programs that have been strategically designed to help students mature in meaningful ways. Section 3 elaborates on some of these programs.

Don't forget to plan for life AFTER a gap year

In the process of planning a gap year, it can be easy to forget that life will go on after the year is over. It is just as necessary to have a plan in place for *after* a gap year as to plan the year itself. While interests and directions may change or develop over the course of the year, having a basic "reentry" plan in place will ensure that students "hit the ground running" when they return. If their plans include attending a college or university, they need to make sure they meet the enrollment deadlines during their gap year, usually in January or early February. Financial aid applications can be submitted as early as October. If a student is already accepted into a school and has deferred their enrollment, they still need to submit FAFSA papers during their gap year, as these decisions are made each year by the school.

After everything a student experiences during a gap year, reconnecting with the "real world" can be tricky. They have likely made deep friendships, perhaps witnessed profound poverty for the first time, and gained a broader understanding of the world than many of their peers. All of these can cause them to reject the triviality they see in other students their age and create a reverse culture shock as they reintegrate into American society. It is important that they understand that this may happen and have a plan to navigate this transition. Many programs do a good job at addressing these issues, but I have seen that the transition is still very difficult. The growth is well worth it, but be prepared for some discontent with their new normal and be ready to encourage your student to intentionally build community as they return home just as they did when they left for their gap year.

WHICH?

Choosing the Right Program

It is encouraging to see a growing number of gap year programs that focus on spiritual development, Christian worldview, service, missions, and leadership development. Some large programs accept over 200 students each year while others have smaller groups. They may use different terminology (i.e., link year, gap year fellowship, walkabout, Bible school) but they all essentially function as gap years. Some programs take place primarily in the U.S., others are strictly international, while still other programs combine both international and domestic experiences.

As you consider a gap year program, it is most important to consider the goals you hope to achieve and choose a program with the appropriate focus, length, location, and price.

Program Focus

All of the programs highlighted here have some degree of focus on spiritual development. Some are focused more on experiential learning and travel while others take a more academic approach; some offer college credit while others do not. Start first by considering your child's personality, interests, and motivations. If they don't enjoy sitting in a classroom, choose a program which focuses more on travel. If, on the other hand, they enjoy intellectual challenges, find an academically-focused program. Additionally, if your child has a particular skill or hobby they want to focus on, look for a program that allows them to do that.

Length

Most gap year programs last nine months. They are designed to coincide with the typical academic school year. Domestic programs often run on a typical college schedule while international programs generally begin with training in the US before departure to an international assignment. As a result, domestic programs generally allow their students to go home for holidays and breaks while international programs do not.

In addition to nine month programs, there are several that last for one semester. In order to create a complete gap year, students could add a second semester of meaningful work or internship.

Location

Students have the option of spending their gap year in the U.S., overseas, or a combination of both. Travel appeals to many students and their natural sense of adventure can motivate them to leave the comforts of home for unknown places. A study of the effects of travel on education reported that 86 percent of college-educated adults admit travel in their youth made them more intellectually curious not only in school but outside of the classroom as well. Almost all of the programs mentioned here have some element of travel, either domestic or international.

Price

Most Christian gap year programs cost between $10,000 and $20,000. This typically covers room, board, travel, and academic instruction (and often includes college credit). Do not let the cost keep you from exploring the value these programs provide. Some accept federal financial aid or allow you to use money from a 529 savings plan. Most programs offer scholarships or will train students in fundraising, which is a great learning experience in itself.

When you consider that one year of college costs between $20,000 and $50,000, a gap year is a good investment. If your child comes out of a gap year with a clearer focus, greater motivation, and a better understanding of the real world, they are more likely to finish college sooner, and this can save thousands of dollars in tuition.

Program guide

The following index is limited to faith-based gap year programs with a Christian worldview. It is not comprehensive in scope nor does it go into great detail about each program. It is designed to expose families to the types of Christian gap year programs that are available. Please visit the websites of each program for more detailed information and/or to arrange visits to programs of interest. For a guide to other gap year programs, I recommend *The Complete Guide to the Gap Year: The Best Things to Do Between High School and College* by Kristin M. White or the website of the Gap Year association.

AIM WORLD RACE GAP YEAR

About the organization

Adventures in Missions is an interdenominational missions organization that focuses on discipleship. Established in 1989, AIM has taken over 115,000 people into the mission field for periods as short as a week up to trips longer than a year. AIM's website states, "We believe that by giving people the opportunity to step outside their comfort zones and join what God is doing in other cultures and nations, lives are transformed."

About the gap year program

The World Race Gap year has experienced explosive growth over the past few years, sending over 250 students per year to almost every continent in the world. Typically, students age 18 to 20 travel to three continents over nine months (September to May) living out of a backpack as they participate in ministries ranging from orphan care, to construction, or to teaching English. Students are placed on a "squad" with 40 to 50 other students and live with mentors at an AIM base in the countries where they serve.

Cost

Program fees range from $16,000 to $18,000 and students are trained and encouraged to raise their funds before leaving on the gap year.

Highlights

- Students can serve in multiple countries and ministries during the nine month program.
- AIM's Parent Vision Trip during month six or seven allows parents the opportunity to visit their student in the country where they are stationed at that point. For our family, this trip was priceless. We met the students and staff that our daughter had spent many hours with, and we were able to participate in ministry with her..

Note

AIM has started a semester-long program that could be incorporated into a DIY gap year plan when paired with meaningful work or other components.

Additionally, AIM offers summer programs for student ages 14 to 18 to the Caribbean, Central and South Americas, Africa, Southeast Asia, and Eastern Europe.

Learn more

Learn more about Adventures in Missions on their website, www.adventures.org and www.worldrace.org. You can also find blogs from current and past team members on these sites. Follow AIM on Instagram @ adventuresinmissions and #worldracegapyear and Facebook @ World Race.

CRU

About the organization

Cru (formerly Campus Crusade for Christ) is an interdenominational Christian organization with more than 25,000 staff in over 170 countries. Their mission is to "win, build, and send, multiplying disciples" with the vision of establishing "movements everywhere so that everyone knows someone who truly follows Jesus". They have been sending college students overseas for both short- and long-term missions for decades.

About the gap year program

In 2018 the first Cru gap year was launched. Students spent two months at Cru's International headquarters in Orlando, Florida being trained and equipped by seasoned ministry leaders before being sent out for three months of ministry in Ecuador and three months of field ministry alongside Cru staff in Kampala, Uganda. Students travel on a team led by experienced Cru staff members and work alongside established high school ministries in other countries. Future routes will vary according to ministry needs.

Cost

The cost of the program ranges from $16,000 to $19,000 and students are trained, coached, and encouraged to raise funds to cover the cost of the program.

Highlights

- Ministry training and support from seasoned missionaries at Cru headquarters in Orlando.
- Students support the work of established ministries overseas that are led by local Cru staff.
- Students receive extensive help raising funds to cover the cost of their gap year.

Note

Cru also offers summer missions opportunities for high school students lasting between two and five weeks and taking place all over the world.

Learn more

Learn more about the Cru gap year @ www.cruhighschool.com/go-global/gap-year and follow the team on Facebook @ Cru Gap Year.

CAMP EAGLE

About the organization

Nestled in the Texas Hill Country, Camp Eagle is an outdoor adventure camp that offers summer camps for kids, retreats throughout the year, and a gap year program.

About the gap year program

The Camp Eagle Wilderness Walkabout gap year focuses on discipleship and teaching students how to be disciples for the rest of their lives. The program is intentionally designed with individual components coming together to form a cohesive nine month discipleship experience. The program includes four major focuses: 25% Adventure, 20% Study, 40% Service, 15% Rest.

The 15 to 30 students in the program spend class time learning how to faithfully read and interpret the Bible. With a strong foundation in Scripture, students move towards critical study of theology to contemplate their own beliefs. Students also move through a survey of diverse world views relevant to our world today. Colorado Christian University offers up to nine hours of college credit to be used at the school of a student's choice. Students who attend Colorado Christian University after the program can earn up to 15 hours.

Cost

The nine month tuition is $10,800. Fundraising is encouraged and financial aid is available.

Highlights

- Students can earn nine to fifteen hours of college credit.
- Nine wilderness expeditions punctuate the year providing a foundation for learning and life application through epic hiking, scenic environments, and thrilling multi-sport adventure.

Note

Camp Eagle also offers a variety of adventure programs and trainings for teens during the summer.

Learn more

Learn more about the camp eagle gap year @ www.campeagle.org/camps/wilderness/walkabout-program/ or follow Camp Eagle Wilderness on Instagram.

HIGHER GROUND

About the organization

Higher Ground gap year is a project of Live 10:27 Ministries in Lititz, Pennsylvania. Higher Ground exists to equip students to discover their callings, own their faith, and build their life's foundation on Christ.

About the gap year program

The three-month program (September-December) focuses on biblical studies, leadership development, career skills, community service, personal finance, and travel. Throughout a semester, students primarily live at camp Higher Ground just north of Harrisburg, Pennsylvania and periodically take trips to other states or countries.

Cost

The three-month program costs $8,500-$9,800 which includes all courses, trips, and room and board. Students are encouraged to fundraise to offset the cost of the program.

Highlights

- Alumni receive a 15% tuition discount to Liberty University.

- Three months, a great option for students wanting to work or intern during their gap year or start school in January.

Learn more

You can learn more about the Higher Ground Gap year program on their website www.highergroundgapyear.com, on Instagram @highergroundgapyear and on Facebook @Higher Ground Gap Year.

IMPACT 360

About the organization

Impact 360 is a project of Lifeshape, a nonprofit organization founded by John and Trudy Cathy White, daughter of Chick-fil-A® founder S. Truett Cathy. After 20 years of working in international missions, John and Trudy recognized an increasing need for equipping young adults in the area of godly leadership. Impact 360 Institute was born out of the vision of Lifeshape to transform communities with the message of Jesus

Christ by equipping young adults to become Christ-centered servant leaders.

About the gap year program

The Impact 360 Fellows experience is a nine-month program offering a unique combination of worldview studies with experiential learning, international travel, and leadership training to over 50 students per year.

"Fellows learn to grow their relationship with God, build intentional community with others, and discern God's call in their lives. Fellows transition into their college experience knowing why they believe what they believe. Being transformed in their character, they are sent out to live a life of Kingdom influence."

Students live on Impact's campus in Pine Mountain, Georgia. The Fellows' experience incorporates both classroom learning and real-life application. During class lectures, Fellows engage with leading Christian scholars and thought leaders on a variety of worldview issues. Fellows apply what they learn by living in intentional community, serving at local non-profits, and supporting missionaries in Brazil during a month-long international experience in January.

Cost

For 2019-2020, the all-inclusive cost per Fellow is $18,200. Financial assistance is available in the form of a grant fund. The average grant for the class of 2018 was an additional $8,000.

Highlights

- Leadership training takes place at Chick-fil-A corporate headquarters in Atlanta, Georgia.
- Tuition discounts given to alumni at seven Christian colleges offer savings up to $18,000 per year.
- Students earn 18 hours of college credit from Union University.

Note

Impact 360 offers two summer programs giving students an opportunity to live on the gap year campus and hear teachings similar to those they would experience during the Fellows program. *Propel* is a one-week student leadership training experience designed for teens who desire to lead and disciple their peers. *Immersion* is a two-week deep dive unpacking the Christian faith which asks the question, Is Christianity actually true and, if so, how can we know that? This experience is designed for any teenage Christian who desires to understand the what and why behind their faith.

Learn more

Visit Impact 360's website @ www.impact360institute.org and follow them on Instagram @impact360fellows or Facebook @ Impact 360 Fellows.

KANAKUK LINK YEAR

About the organization

Link Year is a direct extension of Kanakuk Kamps and follows their mission statement of "Developing dynamic Christian leaders through life-changing experiences, godly relationships, and spiritual training."

About the gap year program

Link Year is a nine-month gap year program located in Branson, Missouri. Link Year students are challenged mentally, physically, and spiritually to grow as young adults. The program focuses on seven areas of growth: Biblical Worldview, Maximizing Moments, Privilege Responsibility,

Heart Transformation, Study of Scripture, Authentic Accountability, and Growing in Gratefulness.

Cost

The 2019 tuition/room/board cost was $15,000. Additionally, each student must take part in an international trip or an internship during the month of February. The cost of these opportunities is not included in the tuition cost.

Highlights

- Students may receive up to 18 hours of college credit through John Brown University after acceptance into their program.
- Kanakuk Link Year also has a basketball development program called Link Hoops. Students participate in link year classes while training and traveling on the team.

Note

Kanakuk has offered summer camps for children and teens since 1926. Attending a summer camp would help give a younger student a good feel for life at Kanakuk.

Learn more

You can find more information about Kanakuk's Link Year @ www.linkyear.com and www.kanakuk.com. Follow them on Facebook @Link Year and Instagram @linkyear.

ONELIFE INSTITUTE

About the organization

The OneLife Institute is an evangelical, Christian organization. As an organization, the staff affirm the historic ecumenical creeds of the church as well as stand alongside the doctrinal statements of their partnering institutions (Cairn University and Southern Wesleyan University).

About the gap year program

OneLife is a nine-month, residential program with four desired outcomes: form Christian character, develop a biblical worldview, increase emotional intelligence, and acquire life skills.

Their four locations — three in Pennsylvania and one in South Carolina — accept 24 to 30 students who earn between 24 and

30 college credits while also participating in both domestic and international trips.

"OneLife exists because we believe that taking a gap year forces students out of the routine of "schooling" and into a deeper relationship with God. Students who participate in gap year programs have proven to be far more prepared for the transition to college and adulthood."

Cost

The cost of OneLife is $22,900 and includes tuition, meals, books, room, board, and all travel expenses. They offer church-matching scholarships, academic scholarships, and FAFSA.

Highlights

- Students earn between 24 and 30 college credits.
- The program offers both domestic and international travel.
- Phone and media use is kept to a minimum to discourage distraction.
- 91% of students receive scholarships to help offset the cost of the program.

Learn more

Find out more about OneLife @www.onelifepath.org or follow them on Facebook @ OneLife Institute or on Instagram @onelife_institute.

SUMMIT SEMESTER

About the organization

Summit Ministries, founded in 1962, aims to train a generation of leaders who understand the times, know what it means to think biblically in every area of life, and who want to be leaders for Christ in their schools, communities, churches, families, and country. Through various extensions, Summit Ministries challenges Christians to develop a biblical worldview and to serve Christ and others by speaking and living the truth.

About the gap year program

Summit Semester combines top-tier academic training in a safe, discipleship-focused environment offering students an extraordinary opportunity for growth and excellence. Students will be taught to worship God with their head (truth), heart (relationships), and hands (practical living). The three-month journey (August-November) starts in the classroom with studies in the areas of Literature, Philosophy, Bible, Ethics, Religion/Worldview, Church History, and Critical Thinking. Students also participate in weekly adventures such as backpacking, exploring, camping, caving, rock climbing, mountain biking, fishing, swimming, and skiing/snowboarding.

Students live in a retreat environment in the San Juan Mountains of Pagosa Springs, Colorado. Over the course of the semester, students are removed from daily life to help them evaluate the culture, themselves, and how they may live out their God-given identities. By taking this time of retreat, students are better prepared to make a difference in the world as they re-engage upon graduation from the program.

Cost

The cost of this 12-week program is $11,495 and covers all classes, food, and lodging but does not include the fee for college credit. Summit Semester offers students the option of receiving college credits through an accredited university. That additional cost is $350 per course.

Highlights

- Students can earn college credits for an additional fee per course.
- Weekly adventures such as backpacking, camping, skiing/snowboarding, fishing and more.

Note

Summit hosts ten two-week conferences every summer at locations including Manitou Springs, Colorado; Union University in Jackson, Tennessee; and Lancaster Bible College in Lancaster, Pennsylvania. Currently, about 2,000 students attend a Summit program each year.

Learn more

Find out more about Summit Semester @www.summit.org/programs or on Facebook @Summit Ministries and Instagram @summitmn.

VOX BIVIUM

About the organization

Vox Bivium is a non-denominational, evangelical Christian gap year school founded by Josh Pederson in 2015. Prior to the founding, Pederson spent 13 years in pastoral ministry including as campus pastor for Grace Church Downtown in Greenville, South Carolina. Vox Bivium has partnerships with multiple Bible-believing ministries and churches that range in denominational ties. Students come from a variety of backgrounds.

About the gap year program

The Vox Bivium Gap Year School in Travelers Rest, South Carolina is designed for high school graduates and college-aged adults who want to gain better clarity and understanding for who they are and what God has called them to do.

Gap year students live at Look Up Lodge, a non-denominational Christian camp, for nine months and spend approximately one week of each month travelling. The program combines mentoring from competent leaders and teachers, experience and adventure, and classroom and hands-on learning all carried out in cooperation with the surrounding community.

Our program provides guidance for those who seek the junction where their "deep gladness and the world's deep hunger meet", where they learn what they most need to do and what the world needs most to have done. This junction, this crossroads, is where Christ calls us.

Cost

Tuition is approximately $18,500 and includes all college credits and tuition, all textbooks, room and board, and travel costs for all trips. Fundraising assistance and payment plans are available.

Highlights:

- One week of travel per month with amazing outdoor adventure opportunities.
- One international trip each year.
- Students can earn 24-30 college credits.
- Students participate in life-skills classes like cooking, auto maintenance, and basic home repairs.
- Students can apply for federal student aid.

Learn more

Read more about Vox Bivium @www.govox.org and follow them on Facebook @Vox Bivium Gap Year School or Instagram @voxbivium

WORLDVIEW AT THE ABBEY

About the organization

Worldview Academy is a non-denominational organization dedicated to helping Christians to think and to live in accord with a biblical worldview so that they will serve Christ and lead the culture.

About the gap year program

Worldview at the Abbey is an extension of Worldview Academy's original vision to empower students to live and think in accord with a biblical worldview. It is designed to equip high school seniors and graduates to lead in a Christ-like way and boldly engage non-Christian worldviews. Students complete two semesters of academic classwork including rhetoric, political science, economics, and applied apologetics. The Socratic classes, leadership and evangelism practicums, and community involvement take place in Canon City,

Colorado. Students also have the opportunity to participate in a whitewater rafting trip, multi-day hiking trips, evangelism in nearby metropolitan areas, and service in local community.

Cost

$18,500 pays for two semesters of housing, lunch and dinner seven days a week, up to 30 hours of transferable college credit, and any mandatory special program fees for white water rafting, camping, and ropes courses activities. Books and breakfast are not included.

Highlights

- Students can earn 30 hours of college credit through Trinity International University.
- Should students choose to continue their education at Trinity International University, they will be automatically accepted upon graduation from the Abbey and will be granted $2,500 per semester in scholarships for the remainder of their time there.

Note

In addition to the gap year program, Worldview Academy offers camps around the country each summer for students ages 13 and up. Attending Worldview Camp gives students an idea of what the year-long program would look like.

Learn more

You can learn more about Worldview at the Abbey @www.worldviewbridgeyear.com or by following them on Facebook @Worldview at the Abbey or on Instagram @wordviewattheabbey.

YWAM

About the organization

Youth With a Mission is an evangelical, interdenominational, non-profit Christian missionary organization. Founded by Loren and Darlene Cunningham in 1960, YWAM's stated purpose is to "know God and to make Him known".

YWAM includes people from over 181 countries and a large number of Christian denominations. Over half of the organization's staff hails from non-Western countries while YWAM boasts over 15,000 full-time volunteers in more than 1,100 ministry locations. They train upwards of 25,000 short-term missions volunteers annually.

About the gap year program

A YWAM gap year consists of two parts. Part one is Discipleship Training School (DTS), a three-month immersion in training and discipleship at a YWAM campus followed by two months of cross-cultural outreach.

In the second part, students participate in the School of Ministry Development (SOMD), a three-month training program that furthers the growth that occurred in DTS and helps students gain direction for how God can use them in the future. SOMD is followed by another two-month outreach that focuses on furthering students' leadership abilities and experiences.

Cost

The cost for the entire ten-month program is $13,590-$18, 810 and includes all food, housing, tuition, and outreach travel. Students can participate in only the five-month DTS phase of the program if they choose. Fundraising is encouraged.

Highlights

- Students can participate in either one or two semesters, each with two months of travel/outreach.

- During the School of Ministry Development, students can choose a specialized area of interest.

Note

YWAM has multiple programs around the world and several US sites that market their DTS program as a gap year. Below you will find links to a few of the many options available through YWAM. The organization also offers hundreds of short-term summer missions trips that could be helpful in getting a feel for the organization.

Learn more

Orlando, FL @www.ywamorlando.org

Madison, WI @www.ywammadison.org

Birmingham, AL @https://www.generationhero.org/gap-year

INGREDIENTS DANCE

About the organization

Michelle Brogan is the founder and director of the Epicenter for the Arts which includes the Dance Revolution national tour and Ingredients Dance Company. She and husband Alec have traveled the country since 2000 teaching students to utilize their gifts and talents for a positive purpose and a higher standard. They envision offering a premiere arts training complex where discipleship, professional instruction, and elite mentoring programs are at the core.

About the gap year program

The Ingredients trainee program lasts from September to May and is based out of the Epicenter for the Arts headquarters in Southlake, Texas. Training consists of character development, biblical application, and daily dance and technique classes where students enhance their skills while learning to evangelize and worship through the art of movement. As a part of the program, participants in ING will work "hands-on" in the ministry of Dance Revolution.

Biblical application classes are held once a week with corporate worship twice a week. Performance opportunities include Dance Revolution National Tour, EarthShakers The Competition, Camp Revolution, various conferences and industrials, holiday and outreach performances, community/street outreach, dance festivals, missions trips, and more.

Cost

The cost for the Ingredients trainee program is $415 per month. The monthly fee does not cover housing, food, or transportation costs, however each year Ingredients' directors find preferred housing for members. Travel to conferences and competition is not included in the monthly cost either and must be covered by the dancer.

Qualifications

Participants are expected to be at an intermediate/advanced level of training and are selected based upon evaluation of a completed application packet, three references, dance audition, and interview.

Highlights

- Participants may attend a local college or university of their choice as long as classes do not conflict with the ING schedule.

- Participants may work as long as scheduling does not conflict with ING schedule.
- Participants will have the opportunity to travel and perform with the Dance Revolution National Tour and at other events and outreaches.

Learn more

For more information about this unique program visit their website @www.ingredientsdanceco.com. You can see the students perform at Dance Revolution conferences around the US, dates are listed @www.dance-revolution.com. Attending one of their 3 day tour workshops will give you a feel for the program and its staff.

WHO?

Student's Stories

Hearing from students who took a gap year may be the most useful way to decide whether a gap year is right for you. The students featured here participated in different programs yet all experienced growth in significant ways and walked away with a deeper sense of who they are, who God is, and how their relationship with Him affects every area of their lives. Many of these stories are taken from their blogs.

EMMA: CRU

The Rooftop

In the evenings in Guayaquil, there's a glorious wind that starts to blow throughout the city. The air is filled with the aroma of roasted coffee beans from the local coffee factory and it feels as if God is giving everyone a break from the continuous perspiration of the day.

At the Seminaro Biblico Alianza where we stayed, we were offered the use of a washing machine on top of the roof. This may seem like an interesting place for doing the weekly laundry, but it worked out well. Most people, from what I've seen, hang-dry their clothes and the rooftop is a perfect place to sun drench your laundry.

It didn't take long for our team to discover that there was much more to this place than washing our daily attire. It's the perfect place to take it all in: the breeze, the picturesque views of the city, and time spent with each other. We even hitched up a few hammocks to take full advantage of the space.

For me, the rooftop was the perfect place to spend time with the Lord. It's quiet peacefulness offered me a place to have conversations with God, cry, and journal. There is an unusual serenity with feeling the breeze and watching the sheets swing into the wind. Despite the chaos of the city around me, the rooftop feels like a special place for me and God to meet.

While in Ecuador, we have been doing a study called *The Seven Realities for Experiencing God* by Henry and Richard Blackaby. We have looked at the story of Moses and what it's like when God invites you into His work. As we ponder what that invitation looks like in our own lives, I've realized that God is always at work and we are always invited to work with him. This has made our time working with high school students much richer because it's not just about my initiation to build relationship with them, I know God is already working in the hearts of those in my midst.

I'm so grateful to be on a gap year with Cru. To have these moments with God is priceless. It has been overdue for me to create more time to seek God's face and to feel His loving presence in my life. To slow down and enjoy the breeze.

BETHANY: DIY

A Focused Passion

My gap year was a time in my life that has forever shaped who I am. When I graduated from high school in 2017, I decided to take a year away from formal schooling and design my own gap year. I wanted to choose the way I would spend my year by combining work, domestic ministry, and international experience. I spent the first semester working at Chick-Fil-A and as an associate for Samaritan's Purse in Boone, North Carolina, and I spent the second semester in the Dominican Republic as an intern with Envision (a ministry through the Christian & Missionary Alliance).

Taking time off of the typical demands of school during my gap year helped me put my passions into focus. If I had not concentrated on serving and using my talents and gifts in a new setting, I would likely have settled for a major in college I was not truly passionate about. My time serving overseas impacted me in countless ways, but perhaps one of the most impactful had to do with communication.

When I arrived in the Dominican Republic, I could not speak Spanish. I love to connect with people and those who know me know I love to talk a lot. So this inability to communicate did a couple things for me. The first is that it quieted my mile-a-minute mouth. This quieting forced me to communicate in different ways. I ended up praying and journaling more than I ever had in my life, and I was shocked by the satisfaction I received from this. It was the first time ever that I used written rather than verbal language to process my thoughts. I also began to pick up on non-verbals and, as I did so, the second thing happened — I began to learn the language.

Communication became something I had to work for. Improvement was slow, but I felt such gratification each time I successfully understood the point of a conversation or sermon. I found that connecting with people was a gift that I had to work to do.

As I returned to the United States, my passion for connecting with people, particularly those from other cultures, was put into focus. I found opportunities at work to speak Spanish with fellow team members and customers. I found that I had a stronger awareness of both my verbal and nonverbal communication and I chose to major in Communication and Spanish because I want to use those things to connect with people around the world in my future career. My gap year helped me sharpen my focus, refine me as a person, and mature me in ways that I never expected.

JOHN WILL: IMPACT 360

Now I Know Who I Am

Growing up, a question frequently circulated in my mind: "Who am I and what am I supposed to do with my life?" It seemed like the whole world had predetermined what I was going to do. It might have had something to do with the fact that I'm 6'6" and live in the heart of the South. My whole life, people have come up to me and simply gawked. "Man, you're tall! Has Coach Saban visited your house yet?" While people meant it innocently, I developed real insecurity in my identity because of this. In the back of my mind, I would think, "If I didn't like sports, wouldn't people think I was a failure for 'wasting' all my height?" It even caused me to question my masculinity. "Was I not enough of a man?" I've always been a gentle, easy-going person but felt that I wasn't as "manly" because I couldn't identify with the "bros".

During my senior year of high school, my parents strongly encouraged me to take a gap year and attend the Impact 360 Fellows Program in Pine Mountain, Georgia. After visiting and interviewing for a spot (mostly to please my parents), I saw the value in the program but felt that it wasn't for me. I didn't really know anyone else doing this sort of thing and hated the thought of doing something different from my peers. When I thought of the phrase "gap year", I honestly just pictured some guy on his Mom's couch playing video games who didn't have any sort of ambition in life. That wasn't me. I had all the answers and was ready to go conquer the world. But God, through a lot of circumstances, softened my heart towards the idea and I ultimately accepted a spot offered to me not really knowing what I was getting into.

To relate all that I learned during my gap year program at Impact 360 would literally take me days on end. It was the first time that I felt completely known by a community of like-minded people who accepted me as I was. I didn't have to put on a mask, hiding behind a facade of what I thought people wanted to see. This gave me the opportunity to be vulnerable and yet still loved me, leading to freedom from mental and spiritual bondage. I had taken Apologetics classes and had grown up in church my whole life so I figured that I would have all the "spiritual stuff" down pat. But I was able to learn about and experience God in completely new ways. The world-class education pushed my thinking and courage to not only share my faith but to know that true biblical faith is not blind and has ample reasons to have confidence in the existence of absolute truth, God, Jesus as the Messiah, and the inerrant Word.

I went to the country of Brazil as a part of the program for a month and got to see God work in and through me in exciting and humbling ways. Just as importantly, I was immersed in a culture different from my own which was so influential for me as I saw that the God I served didn't reside just in America; He truly is Lord of all the nations. But probably the most important thing I learned was that I learned who I was. My whole life I had been searching for the purpose of my life but my own insecurities held me back, leaving me grasping for answers and coming up empty-handed.

For the first time in my life, I not only knew in my head but believed in my heart and soul that my identity was a Child of the Living God who loves me despite my obvious imperfections. He has made me and named me. He defines me, not people, social media, or anything else. My realizing this with fresh perspective totally revolutionized my outlook on life. I further understood this on our several manhood retreats where we learned what it truly meant to be a man of God. Working through my past struggles and doubts relating to masculinity was incredibly liberating.

After graduating from the program, I attended Mississippi College and can now say without any reservations that taking a gap year was the best single decision I could have made for my life. I am more prepared for college and life because of the year I spent with Impact 360. We live in a world today that is more confused and divided than ever before. The world needs young people who know who they are and what they've been created for. A gap year is a once-in-a-lifetime opportunity to start to know, become, and live out who God created us to be.

LYDIA: AIM WORLD RACE YEAR

Black Coffee

I wake up early as the sun breaks through the cracks in the curtains across from my bed and streams across my face in bright, warm streaks. My eyes flutter open as I unzip my sleeping bag and reluctantly stand as my feet touch the concrete floor. I make my way toward the muffled voices I hear from the kitchen as I swing open the bedroom door. I am greeted by fifty of my favorite faces. I weave through my friends playing, laughing, writing as I go to get my cup of coffee and take it outside. I sit on the edge of the house, dig my feet into the red Swahili dirt, and slowly sip my bad, black coffee as the sun begins to warm the ground of a new day.

Black coffee will always bring me back to memories of a simple life. No creamer, no sugar, no artificial addition to what is raw and real. Synonymous with simplicity, my terrible black coffee marked the beginning of a new adventure, a new day living moment by moment alongside people to sweeten the most bitter situations. I believe in living simply.

For nine months, I traveled to three continents and lived in six different countries. My life fit inside one sixty-five liter backpack. I carried my bed, house, pillow, clothes, shoes, books, journals, pens, pictures and letters from home on my back. It was all I had, and I couldn't have imagined needing anything more. From Swaziland to Lesotho, India to Nepal, and Nicaragua to Guatemala, I carried all I needed on my back and beside me in the people that were my family. I found joy in having less. I found the most contentment in having the least amount of stuff, in having dirty feet, and in drinking black coffee.

My first home on my nine-month journey was Swaziland, a landlocked country in South Africa. The fifty people I lived with shared a building with two bedrooms, three bathroom stalls, one sink, two showers, and a small kitchen. Our pantry consisted of peanut butter, corn flakes, bananas, and long-life milk. For a week or so I didn't have electricity, and when the sun set in the early afternoon I practiced living, showering, and cooking only by the light of my headlamp. We travelled on to each country in the same manner, sometimes with more and sometimes with less, but always living simply.

Through the lifestyle I lived I learned many things, like how close you can become when you share daily life with people in unfamiliar places. The bond we experienced through not always knowing what was next, by living in the moment and not a second ahead was life altering. My close relationships with the people around me helped me to realize more than ever before the beauty of individuality. With the fake, pretending, excessive possessions, and choices aside, I found myself. Expectation became my enemy, and flexibility my best friend.

I believe in living simply. I believe that life, like black coffee, is best served unrefined, raw, and real. The best things in life are discovered when the excess is taken away, leaving me to find beneath it who I really am, what I value, and the way in which I see the world. All I need is the people I love, the world to learn from, and the God who created it all to lead me.

LUCAS: CAMP EAGLE WALKABOUT

The Hard Edge Of Beautiful Spaces

At the age of eighteen I found myself in West Texas with twenty or so other young adults who were also trying to figure out life. We were all a part of Camp Eagle's gap year program entitled Walkabout. Before my time at camp, I didn't see much value in the wilderness. I had gone camping a few times growing up out of obligation to a church or family outing, and had fished occasionally but hated every minute of it. The outdoors made me uncomfortable, and I viewed the wilderness as an unnecessary discomfort that had nothing to offer me. I was blind to the true value of the wilderness until I was forced into it. I had never really been an outdoorsman nor had I wanted to be. Regardless, I had to be one for the next nine months at camp. Throughout these long nine months I would find myself again and again at the end of my own strength. I would always end up fuming with anger at my lack of control in the wilderness on backpacking trips. I was constantly frustrated by the lack of convenience and comfort that the wilderness offered. This taught me a very important lesson: The Wilderness forces us to depend on God. I walked into the wilderness as a skeptical, cynical, and defeated teenager. I walked out of the wilderness as a man who had experienced the glory of God through letting go and allowing God's hand through the wilderness to shape me.

EVELYN - VOX BIVIUM

My dream college rejected me, and I'm so glad they did. What was most embarrassing became my biggest blessing. As a senior in high school, I believe I heard, "where are you going to college?" about a thousand times. The right answer, of course, is living on campus at the big university. Right? I was honestly worried though. I knew that I didn't have the grades to get in. I had been lazy about school my senior year. Its called Senioritis. (It is a real thing ok? Look it up on Google.) I didn't even have a good idea about what I wanted to do with the rest of my life. To be honest, I was way overwhelmed about going off to college, but I was also underwhelmed about the idea of staying at home and going to a smaller school. So, me being me, putting off things until the last minute decide that college just isn't right for me. Thank goodness my Mom has my best interest at heart.

My mom had a pamphlet on a gap year school located in Travelers Rest, SC called Vox Bivium. It means "the voice at the crossroads." What is a gap year school? It's a nine month program for high school graduates and college age young adults who need clarity in understanding who they are and what God has called them to do. It allows students to take 24 hours of college credit classes while interning in careers that interest them. It also teaches life skills such as health and physical fitness, cooking, car maintenance and financial budgeting. What's special about Vox? Most of the classes are a deep dive into different perspectives of the Bible, and every 4th week of the month, our class went on an adventure or mission trip in an effort to learn more about each other, the world around us and our creator. We were required to do volunteer work around the school and the city, and we were encouraged to attend a local church service on Sundays. The added bonus were the awesome relationships that grew along the way, starting off as strangers and ending in a family I will always be a part of. But especially my relationship with the Lord. From kayaking Lake Jocassee to hiking the Moab desert. Feeding the homeless in a Philly subway and working with a mission team in Costa Rico. These experiences gave me an opportunity to become the best version of myself.

Growing up in the South, it's quite common to attend church every Sunday with your family. I know I did. It is almost like a routine. But I never felt close with God. I just knew Him, and believed in Him because that's what you're supposed to do. I didn't have a real relationship with Him. But the past nine months changed all that. I now talk to Him, I pray to Him, I yell at Him, I ask Him questions and I know that HE has a plan, even though I may have a plan, too, His always seems to be better than mine. He has my best interest at heart. He knows who I really am. I am more Christ-like because I now feel His presence every day. I have honestly become a better person. I care for other people, I try to be my best, and when I fail, I ask Him to forgive me, because I am not perfect. I am a sinner. And I don't deserve His love and especially His mercy. None of us do! But aren't you glad He is such a good father? He never gives up on us. Romans 5:8 says - "But God showed his great love for us by sending Christ to die for us while we were still sinners." I am so grateful for my experience at Vox, and I know God was walking right alongside me while I was on my great adventure, and He still is. I know He will always guide my footsteps.

REID - ONE LIFE

It was the year 2013 and I was graduating high-school in just a few months. My plan: go to college, study business, start a business, make a ton of money, and live the American dream. This was my legitimate plan. After all, this plan was praised by this world and made sense logically. My motives were seemingly pure – I wanted to get married, raise a strong family, and I wanted to one day "deny my wife nothing that her heart desired". Well, fast forward just 6 months and suddenly everything begins to change.

Through a series of events, I decided to participate in a Gap Year program called OneLife. OneLife really only attracted me because of the travel, adventure, and hands-on learning style. The other thing about OneLife that attracted me was that I received 30 college credits for the year. As I was processing my next steps, I thought, "I can do this program, have a ton of adventures, and transfer into business school without a delay to my aspirations." This was true, however little did I know my entire way of living would be altered.

Three months into OneLife I quickly realized my heart was full of vanity. It was evident through the strong community and the hands-on learning that the Proverb, "the heart of a man plans his way but the Lord establishes his steps" is in fact true. "Who am I to think I can plan every detail of my life and think I have the correct plan?" This is a question I was faced with in my time at OneLife and it was questions like these that changed the way I live my life today. The small, tight knit community, and the focused biblical training are what God used to alter my heart and my mind. For someone who does not particularly like sitting in a classroom, the travel and experience helped keep me engaged and focused on learning and growing. As my time in OneLife continued I developed the strongest friendships I have ever had – one of those lifelong friendships became my beautiful wife.

Fast forward 5 years; I still struggle with wanting what this world has to offer. However, the key word to this statement is that I *struggle*. I see that the desires of my heart are not what will bring fulfillment and it is evident that God has called us to pursue character, surround ourselves with a positive and Christ-centered community, and connect our calling to God's purpose of "going and making disciples".

RECOMMENDED READING

Barna group report on Gen Z

You can order the 2018 Barna report made in cooperation with Impact 360 or listen to the webcast by going to Barna's website shop @ *https://shop.barna.com/products/gen-z*

12 Huge Mistakes Parents Can Avoid: Leading Your Kids to Succeed in Life by Dr. Tim Elmore

Growing Leaders founder Dr. Tim Elmore is passionate about understanding the emerging generation and helping adults teach them how to become leaders in their schools, their communities and their careers. As a youth leadership expert and thought leader in his field, he educates adults to help them understand the challenges and experiences today's generation faces and connect with them in a way that resonates. Dr. Elmore believes, by cultivating leadership abilities in young adults and encouraging the adults who guide them, Growing Leaders can be the catalyst for emerging generations that will truly change the world.

Homeschooling for College Credit by Jennifer Cook De Rosa

Jennifer Cook DeRosa is the foremost authority on earning college credit in high school. Her book explains how the process works, how it benefits students, and will save families thousands of dollars. She also moderates a very active facebook group by the same name. This book is a must read for parents of homeschool high school students. By applying the principles in the book a student can take a gap year and still enter college ahead of their peers.

Consumer Reports, August 2016

www.consumerreports.org/student-loan-debt-crisis/lives-on-hold/

The cover of this issue of Consumer Reports features the story titled: "I Kind of Ruined My Life By Going to College." It shares the findings of a March 2016 Consumer Reports National Research Center survey to those with student loan debt.

Here's what they found:

— 45% of those with student loan debt said college was not worth the cost. (38% of those respondents didn't graduate from college. They're paying for a degree they never received.)

– 69% indicated they had trouble making loan payments.

– 78% earn less than $50,000 per year.

– 43% didn't get any help from parents making financial aid decisions.

It is a sobering article that helps families realize the potential dangers of student loans.

RECOMMENDED WEBSITES

In addition to the excellent websites associated with each gap year program mentioned in this guide, these sites offer additional information that may be helpful to you.

For general gap year information and program listings: www.gapyearassociation.org/

To help your student make wise and informed decisions about their future: www.5majorsteps.com

Tim Elmore's excellent blog on understanding and leading the next generation of leaders: growingleaders.com/blog/

To learn how to earn college credit in high school: www.homeschoolingforcollegecredit.com

ABOUT THE AUTHOR

LeAnn Gregory spent the last 25 years mentoring college students in the US and abroad with the campus ministry CRU. Through her work at Auburn University, Appalachian State University and The University of Zagreb, Croatia, she walked alongside hundreds of students as they made life changing decisions about their futures. She realized that many could have benefited from making more informed decisions before investing thousands of dollars in a college education. As a result, she is passionate about helping students prepare for their next steps after high school - whether it be college, a gap year, entrepreneurship, or other pursuits. Her *5 Major Steps*

curriculum and workshops encourage students to investigate their strengths, interests and aptitudes so that they can create a career plan based on broad exploration and informed choice.

Two of LeAnn's 3 teenagers have participated in gap year programs, with the third planning to do a gap year when she graduates from high school. In 2018 she helped CRU launch their 1st gap year program which gives students training and ministry experience on 3 continents. She has counseled many families about gap year options and wrote *The Gap Year Guide* to help even more families understand the benefits of faith based gap year programs.

LeAnn is available to speak at conferences and events on the topics of high school planning, career guidance, and the benefits of faith based gap year programs for teens. You can contact her at TheGapYearGuide@gmail.com.

Special thanks to Yogi Collins for her expertise and encouragement in the process of compiling this guide.

Made in the USA
Columbia, SC
23 April 2021